# Mother Mary Ponders

## The 14 Stations of the Cross in the Experience of Mary, our Blessed Mother

Meditations by Sr. Teresa Joseph Patrick of Jesus and Mary, OCD

These meditations, written in 1988, were first published in the book,
*Personalizing Russia, Even by Those Who Knew Her Little but Who Love Her Much* (volume II), published by the Carmelite Monastery of St. Therese in Gilmore, Quezon City.

By choice in the first printed edition,   the illustrations on the front and back covers are icons from ancient Russia as culled from the book, *Ikon: Inspired* Art, published by the Wijenburg Foundation, the Netherlands. Cover art Four Passion Scenes, Russian (Moscow), 17th century, 45 x 38 cm

Back cover art *Mother of God Hodegetria*, Asia Minor, ca. 1700, 87 x 65 cm

First Publisher: Gabriel Books, 1988



---

[1] This  second edition commemorates the 101st  earthly life of the author who celebrated her birthday on 28 March 2021, Holy Monday. Cover Art:
https://upload.wikimedia.org/wikipedia/commons/7/7e/Russian_-_Crucifixion_-_Walters_37309.jpg
Back cover art: Image Source:
https://commons.wikimedia.org/wiki/File:Byzantine_School_-_The_Virgin_and_Child_(%27Virgin_Hodegetria%27)_-_RCIN_403492_-_Royal_Collection.jpg

Proceeds of the sale of this digital edition, net of development and related costs, shall go to the Carmelite Monastery of St. Therese 4 Gilmore Ave., Quezon City, Philippines

# Introduction

Mary, our Blessed Mother, accompanied Jesus on the road to Calvary. Jesus has left us all, all mankind, in the care of Mary. In the power of His Resurrection, Jesus gives us Mary, through the Holy Spirit, in Mother Church who has become Mater et Magistra, our Mother and Teacher.

Christ is still being incarnated in all men to the end of time. Mother Church brings forth "Christs" through the sacrament of Baptism, matures them through the anointing of the Holy Spirit through the sacrament of Confirmation and nourishes them through the Body and Blood of our Eucharistic King and the Word of God.

All human beings are made in the likeness of Jesus Christ; and this one life is given us so that through God's love and mercy, and the cooperation and free will of men, we can actualize Christ in our lives through the Spirit.

The key to this actualization is Mary's Fiat. The pattern of holiness we are asked to follow derives from the pure faith in loving obedience of Mary in the total surrender of her life to the mysterious will of the Father.

Therefore like Mary, our Mother, we each must commit ourselves to carrying out
God's holy will for each of us. To be able to live like Mary, God gives each of us a cross to carry lovingly because the cross symbolizes total surrender.

Yet this cross, which is suffering in all forms and for all reasons, is not really meant to be carried out, but to be lived out in full faith, hope and love daily.
Mary has shown us the way.

Mother Church guides, protects us and sustains our strength in faithfulness to Jesus our Saviour and Redeemer.

We trust that a prayerful reflection and meditation on these 14 Stations can deepen our love of Our Lady and so understand more penetratingly how Mother Church-the whole Mystical Body of Christ-continues this pilgrimage through time and until the Second Coming of Christ.

*Deo gratias*. ~ Sr. Teresa Joseph Patrick of Jesus and Mary, OCD, Manila, Philippines 1988

# The 14 Stations of the Cross

## Prologue

Mary had spent a quiet night. She had come home tired. Two of her neighbors had needed help. She was glad to be home at last, especially for her Son's need. But He was not home.

The moon was full. She had waited for Him, sitting up all night, as she had been wont to do. But she had not been anxious. This had been Jesus' way. He would not come home now and then. The years had made her understand that deeply. He must be about His Father's business!

So after breakfast, she went to get that seamless robe, to sew on it a hook she felt was needed. But where was it? She was sure she had put it there, intending to finish it today. Suddenly a thought struck her. Did He get it? Was it for this night?

## I. JESUS IS CONDEMNED TO DIE

A crowd of friends has come, rushing to her. "Mary, come! Come with us! Have you not heard.  Jesus has been taken prisoner? They've tortured Him. He is there now , before Pilate!"

"Abba, Father!" Mary prayed in her heart. In her depths, she knew the time had come! Without a word, she went out with her friends.

Let us go back a few days before, into the heart of Mary. Spoused to the Holy Spirit since the Annunciation, whenever the Father wants her to get a little courage, a little strength, Mary receives glimmering lights, understanding the reality confronting her. These lights are given to her in the Word; then the Spirit comes to her, in her constant pondering of the gifts of the Father in her.

So that after three years of the public ministry of Jesus, during which time the Spirit had confirmed in her the holy mission of Jesus, she had been given to understand how she would be united to Him heart and soul. The Spirit thus prepared her gradually—through the many trials of detachment and transcendence given her-to know the great trial that would be His and hers.

A few days ago, the same Spirit had intimated to her that Jesus would need a seamless robe. So one day she was found by Jesus doing this robe. Now and then, Mother and Son would look at each other knowingly. Both seemed to know. The depth of their communion, in their measureless love for the Father's will, kept them one in that silent commitment to all that would soon happen. And so that was how, from the sympathetic disciples and followers–Mary, alone in her house, was finally informed that Jesus had been taken from the Garden of Gethsemane and had been condemned to death.

She had spent hours in pure prayer to the Father for His Son. It was mid morning, around 10:00, when she finally went to Pilate's palace. From afar, she saw a crowd that was becoming unruly. The people she passed by made way for her.

Each looked at her with great sorrow and anxiety.

She heard their whispers: "He had been scourged and was all bleeding." And immediately she felt her whole body mercilessly whipped and lacerated, her heart pierced by many stabs. She was brought to her depths in confusion and anguish.

She heard further: "They have pressed a crown of thorns on His head that now bleeds profusely. They have mocked Him, scourged Him, spat upon Him!"

Each bit of awesome news struck her down to her very depths and she felt helplessly and hopelessly powerless. Was she going to faint? But in those depths, she found the reassuring words of the Father: "Fear not, it is I."

She pressed on forward once more in newfound strength. She had been reassured: "I the Spirit am with Jesus, He is possessed of a great love. Fear not!"

GLORY BE TO THE FATHER, THE SON AND THE HOLY SPIRIT!

## II. JESUS TAKES HIS CROSS

Mary could not get any nearer anymore, even as some in the crowd recognized her. The women by her side did not want her to advance farther. Mary Salome and Mary, the mother of Zebedee's sons, asked her to just stay on there—just to be! To go no farther. In that she found the Father's next word: "Be!"

Immediately she was stilled. In her heart she knew that the Scripture was being fulfilled-yes, He'd have to carry the cross! But how truly heavy was it? How far would He have to carry it?

Full of these unasked questions, again the Word welled up in her: "Mary, my child, be!" And again she felt comforted by the stillness that was the Father's instant gift.

GLORY BE TO THE FATHER, THE SON AND THE HOLY SPIRIT!

## III. JESUS TAKES UP HIS CROSS

Lost in contemplation of the Word, caught up in the love of the Father, suddenly she heard shrieks from the crowd. A piercing shriek, then unbelievable groaning from the onlookers. From Jesus' own disciples: "He has fallen! He has stumbled with His cross! Is He dead? Can He still get up?".

She heard this distinctly in her heart, "Father, Abba, Father." This was all Mary could say, repeatedly. Her whole being crushed, she felt she too had fallen beneath the cross. And she felt herself also crying out: "Abba, Father, Abba, Father: Your Son!"

And as she lay prostrate in spirit, unable to move or open her eyes, peace descended once more into her soul.

And she heard: "He's up now. He's going on--still with the cross!" She found herself praying to the Father: "O Lord God, give Him strength, have mercy."

But the followers of Jesus were also saying this out loudly. Louder and louder. the noise was getting closer and closer to Mary. She also started to move on, almost being bodily carried by the women on her side.

Then suddenly she felt a presence getting closer. A fresh whiff of air was coming then; the crowd was parting; people seemed to be going toward her or making room for her. So she craned her neck a bit to see where Jesus was.

And there! There she saw-first, the Roman soldiers big, husky, cruel looking, helmeted men with whips—"God almighty, who is it they are giving lashes to?" She heard that clearly. Then she got a glimpse of her Son, almost bent double, dragging a massive crossbeam on his back. She could see no farther, she was going to faint. This was yet the cruelest sight in her life.

GLORY BE TO THE FATHER, THE SON AND THE HOLY SPIRIT!

## IV. JESUS MEETS HIS MOTHER

Then suddenly the small group of men, the center of this procession of hate, was approaching her, where she stood. Her Son was going to see her! "O Father, Abba, Father. Let Him come to me. Let me comfort Jesus! Father, give me His cross. Father, let me carry the cross with Him!"

All this unspoken. Agony twisted her whole being and crushed her into a pulp of flesh and blood. Scarcely able to open her eyes, she strained to see—swallowing the distance between her and her Son. Now rushing forth, gently struggling to free herself from the loving arms that held her, and thus restrained, she heard the Father's word anew—"Mary, my child, be still!"

And instantly she was composed. Instantly she knew—this is all part of what must be. *FIAT!*

She was now strong again-strong as a rock, a fortress! She stood firm, her whole being full of light. Her strength was coming from her depths, as though now that Jesus was within a meter from her-suddenly the Father was there! Saying to the two of them—"This, because no one must be lost. This must be because it has to be! Evil and death have to be vanquished!"

They were a threesome at that very moment: Chronos was Kairos. Time and eternity made one!

Mother and Son looked at each other, and they knew! Wasn't the Father holding both of them—a hand on each head? It was clear—and they both knew—and in their hearts again, both said: *FIAT.*

GLORY BE TO THE FATHER, THE SON AND THE HOLY SPIRIT!

# V. SIMON OF CYRENE HELPS JESUS WITH THE CROSS

The crowd was hushed. Why did not Mary remonstrate? How could Mary just look at her Son that way? Why didn't Jesus say a word to comfort His mother? Or His mother to comfort Jesus? Why did they just look at each other? But that mutual gaze spelled their heavenly destiny-they both knew!

And Mary afterwards had suddenly become composed, deeply quieted. Now she walked alone, dignified in her grief. Eyes cast down, she pressed her veil and mantle about her as though to keep most secret what had transpired between her and her Son!

And out of that beautiful quiet and composure, she heard a sigh that went like fresh water given in benediction-she felt blessed.

Then from nowhere she heard: "Someone has offered to help Him carry the cross! Look, the soldiers have pulled a man and forced him to help Jesus!"

This she heard like an hosanna! In her heart, she knew he*r Fi*at had delighted the Father and He had sent relief. She knew that all she could do from now-as always the Spirit had taught her- was to let go: "Mary, accept all that happens. The Father knows what he is doing."

She had become more deeply rooted in faith. The Father's face has been slightly unveiled.

Now she stands: as the pillar of courage and steadfast love. In her heart, she is determined to fix her whole being on God, the Father!

GLORY BE TO THE FATHER, THE SON AND THE HOLY SPIRIT!


## VI. VERONICA WIPES THE FACE OF JESUS[2]


And again, a gasp-she felt this is a reward. What was it? What had happened?


Why has that gasp of admiration now turned into anxious excitement? She looked around, wondering what again lost, unhinged again from the Father's face. "He gave the woman the imprint of His own face!" The voices were grateful, awed, reverent.


She was aghast-all was so strange. Now she asked more openly— "What happened now, please?" She asked the woman beside her. And full of wonderment and joy, they told her as in a chorus-a woman-was it Veronica? Yes, Veronica had boldly stepped forward and wiped His face! Full of blood and sweat! And He had rewarded her: that towel bore the face of Jesus! Preciously, it bore the face of Jesus!


Her heart leaped for joy! How wondrously generous the Father is! How greatly He rewards those who are good to Jesus. And deep, deep gratitude welled up in her for Veronica. And, too, all the kind souls were happy with her at that gladsome news.

---

[2] https://www.newadvent.org/cathen/15362a.htm

Mary knows all over again that the Father was there—is there
with them! And for Jesus, what a relief! What comfort that
beautiful thoughtfulness gave Him! Mary is certain that Jesus
is reassuring His followers: "Love is rewarded by Love." And
for a little while, Mary's heart is suffused with sweetness until-
there! Again, what shrieks! Her heart suddenly, once more
ruthlessly, mercilessly lacerated! Agonizing cries heard all
around!

GLORY BE TO THE FATHER, THE SON AND THE HOLY
SPIRIT!

**VII. JESUS FALLS THE  SECOND TIME**

"He has stumbled again!" He has fallen! O God, He must be
dead!"

"Father, Abba, Abba, Father! Have mercy on Your Son!

She was thrown into the abyss of agony once more! She almost
collapsed. The two women by her side felt her weight heavy on
their shoulders, and they too had shuddered. They could not
console her, for Mary looked as one dead. No word from her,
no groaning. Her eyes were firmly closed.

She was white as sepulcher and totally unmoving. In her
depths, she was on the knees of her heart. She was prostrate
before the Father. Here now, she was totally offered: no word,
no thought, time had stopped.

She had let go-"Do with me what You will. Glory to You!
Abba, Father.

No need to understand. Suffering and sufferer are one. She was there: Jesus Himself beneath the cross. They could not kill her with any greater, damning cruelty! This was to be the ultimate. Her soul melted in a consuming *Fiat*.

How long did she lie prostrate in spirit, inert as though unfeeling? Time no longer existed—this was the end. She felt the weight of the world's faithlessness and sin. It was indeed too much for her.

GLORY BE TO THE FATHER, THE SON AND THE HOLY SPIRIT!

## VIII. THE WOMEN OF JERUSALEM WEEP OVER JESUS

But what now? "No, it doesn't seem so. They say He has become stronger. There! He is eager to meet the crowd! Yes, Mary. look, look. Yes, Jesus is actually talking, talking to the women. Quick, let's get to Him. Mary, see, look! He's up and strong! And yes, there He is addressing the women and children!

It was as if new life has oozed into her from nowhere—from Jesus perhaps. Why, Mary herself was suddenly so strong again-and "Yes, yes, come please, hurry. Let's see! What is He telling them? O merciful Father, Deo gratias, Deo gratias!

Mary had scarcely reached the place, two meters from Jesus, when again He was moving on. But now again, why does He look so very, very weak? He was almost on His knees. He was almost crawling! "O Father, Abba, Father-enough! Enough, we beg of You!"

Mary was groaning anew. But the followers of Jesus were just reaching her now to hear Jesus' comforting words to the women: "Mary, Jesus said for them not to weep for Him. No, but weep for themselves and for their children."

So this was what He was saying to them? Mary was stunned! She remained transfixed and the Spirit comforted her "My beloved, don't you understand? Jesus is beyond all defeat! Weep not for Him. He will soon be glorified. Mary, all this is only for a moment now—and He will be sitting on the Father's right hand in heaven. Mary, have you forgotten?"

The Spirit enfolded her once more, and the Father cupped her heart in His almighty hand. And so Mary prayed immersed in the heart of the Spirit: "Never let me question. Never let me cry out! Forgive me! Forgive me!"

GLORY BE TO THE FATHER, THE SON AND THE HOLY SPIRIT!

## IX. JESUS FALLS THE THIRD TIME

"He's finished! He's dead! He has fallen! He's finished! He's gone!" She heard this. Like a wave of death's poison, the news got around fast.

But Mary had just been purified for all else to come. The Spirit had totally transformed her anew. From here on, Mary was to become totally woman, no longer mother, totally child to the Father, totally spoused to the Spirit.

She had become a warrior in battle array. So the news got in more clearly now and it now became for her like a report merely. "No, Jesus still lives but He can no longer carry the cross. Look, He is down! He cannot get up! O Mary!"

In her heart, she kept saying, *"Fiat,* Father. Thy will be done. Is this the end, Father? Father, take Him to Yourself!" She groaned in the Spirit and gradually peace came upon her. She had become totally spiritualized as though she no longer was a feeling, sorrowing mother.

Time had stopped again. For a moment. she was just not there, but for how long? Who knows? But then...

GLORY BE TO THE FATHER, THE SON AND THE HOLY SPIRIT!


## X. JESUS IS STRIPPED OF  HIS GARMENTS

"Oh, no, no, no!" The women from afar were shouting. "Oh, no, but His flesh is coming off too as they tear His garments from the drying blood on His body! O Lord, no, have mercy!"

Mary clutched the arms of the women holding her, her face contorted with grief. Yet she stood upright, her face fixed on heaven. In her heart, she knew every pain in that mangled body, every fiber of His muscle. For were these muscles not of the very body she had wiped with dry cloth whenever He had a slight fever? All over again, now as if she were an island apart, her memory now totally possessing her, she recalled all the loving motherly ministrations she had given the body of the child Jesus. And now she realized that the garment they were pulling off His body was that seamless robe she had just made for Him.

Of course, everything must go. It was only right, she thought- and while she was being lulled along by those reminiscences, she heard agonized shouting again.


GLORY BE TO THE FATHER, THE SON AND THE HOLY SPIRIT!

## XI. JESUS IS NAILED TO THE CROSS

And without telling her clearly what they were doing to Him, she suddenly knew! This was yet her wildest, most tormenting pain! It flashed clearly before her. The soldiers had rudely, cruelly, ruthlessly broken His body.

Jesus had collapsed, so bent double, almost permanently, by the weight of the cross. They found it easy to rudely and cruelly stretch Him out, pressing that stooping curved back flat on the cross. His bones breaking, she heard them, she felt them. So now He lay stretched out on the cross as one completely dead.

In her heart now, she clearly saw what they were going to Him. All those heavy iron nails—so very long and black. They were hammering them on His wrists between the palm and the lower forearm. Yes, they were hammering, pounding then down, each one on His quivering hand.

With velvety touch, those were the hands that she and Joseph had kissed so lovingly. Those hands had grown calloused and beautiful like Joseph's—they were a carpenter's hands—but still delicate and consecrated.

As she heard the hammering, she was being hammered too in her very heart. The nails were being hammered into her heart!

Now they began to pound the nails into His two feet. All this she saw clearly in her mind's eye, in her heart fully surrendered to the Father.

Suddenly she felt she was being lifted up in spirit, up and beyond all this by a Power she only knew was now there and was dominating her whole being. She too was nailed down on the cross in her heart.

No, she was not being lifted up. She was there being nailed with Jesus, feeling every bit of that nameless, indescribably agonizing, mind-exploding pain. Yet her heart was still. The abyss of quiet, total confidence possessed her: all was given, totally surrendered!

The Spirit had kept her in the bosom of the Father, in some
way, so that she was both in pain and out of it. She was both
now and at the same time in another, in time and in eternity,
mortal and immortal! She was nowhere. She had become all
creation sundered. The universe had darkened.

GLORY BE TO THE FATHER, THE SON AND THE HOLY
SPIRIT!


## XII. JESUS DIES ON THE CROSS

No, the crowd could not go on. No, the soldiers were
prohibiting the people from getting closer. But Mary and the
women were still quite a distance away. They could walk a
little faster perhaps because they could see that they were
bringing the cross farther on, to the very top of the hill.

And now with newfound strength and fresh new courage—
where did she get this?–Mary urged the women and the few
disciples with her: "Let's go on faster. Come quickly-see Him!"
Where did she get this strong drive, these eager feet that now
stepped lightly but firmly up the hill?

And behold the soldiers were anticipating her, it seemed. They
seemed actually to be waiting for them. Yes, yes, they were
allowing her and a few women. Oh, and only one man to go
with them, only John. And yet when she looked around for the
other disciples, they were really nowhere in sight. So Mary
said:

"Let it be. If only John, let it be. *We* must get there." So the
little procession steadily walked with Mary's newfound
strength.

The women were amazed and now they stood beneath-the horror of horrors! Jesus was truly hanging on that cross. His body sagged, buoyed up only by those nails, blood oozing from those hammered hands and feet, His hair caked in blood hanging down his blood-sweated gruesome face, His whole body racked by now and then spasms of uncontrollable pain. But she heard Him loud and clear in her heart. Jesus had begged forgiveness for his torturers.

The air was becoming rarefied: a Presence was there whom Jesus was addressing. Yes, she heard Him too as He spoke to the thief beside Him: "This day, thou shalt be with me in Paradise!" The man pulped and crucified spoke with power! She knew it was true!

This is God's own Son, even as He looked more like a worm than a man. Despite His grotesque figure contorted by the sin He had taken upon Himself,  there was an awesome dignity and palpable transcendent mystery surrounding this one particular figure on the cross. It was as though the whole, now darkening, crumbling universe, was only lighted by this one radiantly glowing, blood spattered cross.

Jesus kept His eyes down all this time as the little group looked up agonizingly, silently at Him. And then suddenly, as though indeed master of this whole being and of the whole universe, He raised His head! He opened His eyes and fixed them straight ahead, beyond the whole spectacle as though piercing the very horizons of heaven.

And then He turned His gaze downwards, first to His mother. He knew exactly where she stood. And then He gazed at His beloved disciple John. And in that sepulchral silence, in a voice that did not seem to come from Him, because it sounded in Mary's heart, she heard: "Woman, behold your son," and He looked long at this woman, His mother to whom He was leaving all.

Then He turned to John, but without the old familiar lightsome glint of loving look that John always knew was His loving sign for him. But now suddenly sounding imperial but paternal, and beyond time, He said: "Son, behold your mother." And He looked at him and beyond him, as though to have that message endure for all peoples through all the ages.
Then He looked down once more and, for the rest of that scene, had become suddenly wrapped up in a mystery of being in which Mary could no longer share.

He was now all alone. Now He and the Father communed. Mary felt that Jesus was being consoled by the Father. But all of a sudden, she heard Him cry: "Lami, *lami. Sabachtha*ni! My God, my God, why hast Thou forsaken me?"

It was a cry that shook the very heavens! It was a lamentation never, ever to be heard again from man. The whole cosmic universe was wrung dry and uprooted from its moorings. The heavens darkened. Flashes of lightning ribboned the sky, Billows of clouds were shot through with thunderous rumblings. The very earth groaned. All Calvary seemed caught up in the desolation of the Son of God!

Mary was no longer Mother, she had become fully Woman. She was crushing the head of Satan at that very moment, not through her power—the power was coming from the cross. And it came to her in a full but slow way.

"I thirst." No, that was not a shout. It was Jesus' loving cry. He was crying for souls! It was a cry of unceasing, deep desire for the Father's joy and the salvation of souls.

He now sees clearly the mission His Father had given him-souls! And full of the Father's own thirst now, Jesus pronounces the enduring permanent longing, recognized or not, by every single created human being the quest for God. His thirst for souls has become all creation's thirst for God which only those graced and purified and honest will readily identify as thirst for the living but hidden God.

All this has also become clear to Mary, The fount of this total desire, Christ's thirst, has become hers. And it has become the thirst of Holy Mother Church, Mary sees now that this is the destiny Jesus announced to her from the cross: to mother souls through the Church. She is now to bring souls to the Father in Christ through the Spirit. He now confirms this in her heart.

And lost in this new seeing, she almost missed Jesus' final and total surrender. Now He is talking to the Father. And Mary hears Him say: "Father, into Thy hands I commend my spirit. Mary now knows the moment of victory has come! Her Son is going home to His Father and her Father. Forever, He will be gone as her Son: this is the final moment of motherly possession.

And she hears it strangely spoken "It is consummated!" And the Spirit of Jesus bursts forth into the heavens! Mary gasps in total wonderment. Heaven and earth are one, life and death are one, man and God are one! And filled with this transparent truth which the Spirit has written across her mind, she is lifted up in spirit. Her Son's words-"It is consummated!"—make her realize in the deepest sense that for her too, her motherhood of the Son is now totally and fully consummated. Finished. Glory be to the Father, the Son and the Spirit--their plans for man's salvation is finished!

What a rest this truth afforded her-filling her whole being with light and strength and so she stood there: royal in bearing, undaunted, straight and rooted in truth, like a pillar holding heaven and earth.

Lost in these triumphs, she failed to see that a soldier had pierced Jesus' side with a lance. And once again, she felt that she had been bathed, dyed and crimsoned in that blood and water that flowed out from Jesus' breast.

That was the most cruel of all, she thought, to pierce and stab Him who already was dead. But the Spirit made Mary see-she was being baptized anew in that blood and water-as Mary Mother of all men, Mother of the Church and of all consecrated souls! The Church is born: the Immaculate made flesh in Mary and now as the Mystical Christ, the Church.

GLORY BE TO THE FATHER, THE SON AND THE HOLY SPIRIT!

## XIII. MARY RECEIVES THE BODY OF JESUS FROM THE CROSS

And now finally, the good men who brought Jesus down from the cross reverently laid His body on Mary's lap and she entered once more into the motherhood of her Son, all over again.

We fall silent.

For is this not the body that had come from her own body? She knew every fiber of each muscle. She traced the features of His now sodden and blood-caked face, clearing it of the clots and blood, feeling gratefully the weight of that unmoving body on her lap.

How much pain and torture can a frail body like that take? But she knows all over again; He has accepted all that to win souls for heaven! And so she stares at this Man, her Son, yet not fully comprehending how the whole of all creation has been given to that vessel of her own flesh and blood. While non-comprehending, Mary comprehended all, in an emptiness of all thought and feeling that has become a fathomless abyss of knowing and not knowing, of peace beyond understanding.

In worship, this is adoration.

For Mary the Mother, all over again, was not there as mother, though her heart was sundered through and through with searing stabs of agonizing sorrow. Yet she was Woman all over who is child to the Father who knows all. And her whole being-racked with uncontrollable grief and pain—was somehow in the total embrace of the Spirit who is the fullness of that depthless, cavernous void.

Mother and Son caught in a timeless moment, like an unmoving sculptured Pieta that was immortalizing love unto death, for all mankind. Long was the silence of that oneness, which like the last utterance of the Son-"It is consummated"— is now closed forever on this earth to resurrect as Mother and Son. As of a past yet transcended beyond personal relationships, in a heaven that awaits now, but only the Mother, who yet must be fully Woman, in and for all her sons, who must crush the serpent's head, crushed once and forever by the heel of the second Eve, Mary! The evil one, the serpent who will nonetheless continue through time to harass the Kingdom of her Son in all men, to the end of time.

And now, Mary coming to the fullness of understanding of the work left by her Son, in what she is now as Mother of the Church, Mary lifts her eyes to the men around her and made a motion also as if to say: It is indeed consummated!

GLORY BE TO THE FATHER, THE SON AND THE HOLY SPIRIT!


## XIV. JESUS IS LAID IN HIS TOMB

The beloved apostle John, delicately respectful of this last togetherness of Mother and Son, now comes eagerly forward to receive a son's benediction from the Mother now made his own: John representing all mankind.

Joseph of Arimathea and Nicodemus and the band of loyal comforters-to whom she had been so deeply grateful came around too. Reverently, lovingly, awed and deeply grieved, moving with an overwhelming sense of mystery and tragedy and personal loss, they lifted the lacerated body from Mary's lap and moved on, gently, to lay Jesus in the tomb that had earlier been prepared.

Left alone, Mary sat still unmoving: her depths gently stirred by a continuous message that was not yet coming through clearly, but which already gave her the fullness of faith. For the Spirit was gently, ever caressingly reassuring her of what Jesus had earlier announced clearly. In three days, He would resurrect: this was going to be!

She had no doubts about it. That was the fullness of the ground of her being, caught up in the unchanging truth which totally possessed her! Jesus had gone home to the Father, dazzlingly beautiful as Eternal Life, in the embrace of the Father in the Spirit.

But this body she now sees: this is something quite unclear, but over which she does not bother much to mind about, because she just knows that Jesus is alive in the realm where He reigns! But how this is to be seen by now all her sons in the Spirit-this body being now being interred-how will this come back? How will it in the tattered flesh as she now sees it in inconsolable grief? Is this to be the same body fully and emblazoningly made whole?

She knew-just as the query passed her mind quietly—she knew it would be made whole. It would be a glorified body! How she knew, we too now know: for she has all the wisdom given her from time to time by her Spouse.

Only in the Spirit does she comprehend all things, even without wishing to comprehend. It is as though she herself has become the truth in the Truth that is her Spouse and Master.

And already, now Mary looked remote indeed to the men who had turned to her anew. Having laid Jesus in the sepulcher, the sepulcher now became the womb she once was of the enfleshed *W*ord. And as though startled by the stark physical truth that now Jesus was going to be sealed up and left in that dark, cold cemented vault. Mary sprang to her feet and rushed into the sepulcher to see Him, her own Son just once more now-she, His mother!

And as she lovingly, grievingly pressed His hands that knew the nails and passed her hands over His deeply quieted face, she planted a last tender delicate kiss on His now again beautiful forehead.

Finally, in the Father's love and through the Spirit, Mary made her last benedictions on that body that lay inert, and now again becoming totally Other even as she knew in her depths-like a radiant light from above-that she had come once more now, not to say goodbye, but Alleluia!

GLORY BE TO THE FATHER, THE SON AND THE HOLY SPIRIT!

Sr. Teresa Joseph Patrick of Jesus and Mary, OCD